The Adventures of Scuba Jack
Copyright 2022 by Beth Costanzo
All rights reserved

It was late in the afternoon and donkey, llama, goat, and duck were happy to see the farmer. He filled up a large tub and added some bubble bath.

All the animals jumped in with a big SPLASH! The animals were thankful for their bath.

After they were done the farmer noticed the goat had a scratch on his leg and bandaged him up. The farmer then brushed all the animals' teeth and curled the llama's hair.

"Time for dinner!" said the farmer. The animals were all thankful for the farmers kindness.

The farmer walked into his house, kissed his wife on the cheek as she lay sleeping in bed for the night.

The farmer was thankful for his wife and loved her very much! He sat in his comfy chair and began to read the newspaper and fell asleep.

he farmer woke with the sound of pans banging together.
e looked up and noticed his kitchen table was nicely set
ith good China. There were streamers hanging on the
iling and a big sign that said, "Thank you!"

His wife walked into the room and was surprised to see the beautiful decorations and breakfast waiting on the table.
"What in the world?" said the farmer.
"Who did all this?" said his wife.

Just then the animals walked into the dining room. "We hope you don't mind, but we made you breakfast." said the duck. "Talking animals?" said the farmer.

"We want to "Thank You" for taking such good care of us, so we wanted to do something nice for you!" said the donkey. "That was so thoughtful!" said the farmer's wife.

"Would you like to join us?"
"We would love to!" said the llama.
"You know its important to always say, "Thank You," said the goat. They finished their meal and the animals offered to clean up the breakfast dishes.

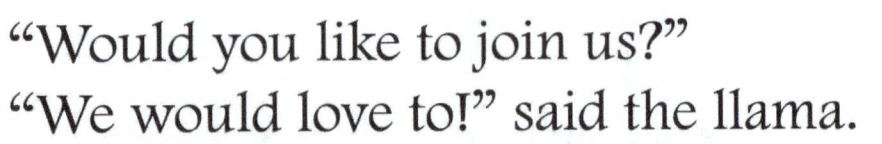

"I think I need to lay down," said the farmer.
"Me too!" said the wife.

One hour later………
The cuckoo clock sounded and woke the farmer and his wife from their nap.
"Maybe this was just a dream?" thought the farmer.
He grabbed his coat and headed out to his truck.

He began driving down the long dirt road toward town. Just then he spotted donkey, llama, goat and duck peeking out from under the blanket in the back of the truck.

"Do you mind if we join you?" said llama. "Oh, ok…." Said the farmer. "Thank you again for taking such good care of us!" said Goat.

"Can we stop for ice cream?" said donkey. "I need to use the bathroom," said duck. "Go faster!" said llama. The farmer looked amazed. He wasn't dreaming! His animals could talk!

The farmer felt "blessed" and "thankful" at the same time. He knew he was very lucky to have these new, unusual friends. Goat, llama, duck, and donkey were equally grateful to have the farmer in their lives and were always "thankful" for his kindness.

www.ingramcontent.com/pod-product-compliance
Lightning Source LLC
Chambersburg PA
CBHW060429010526
44118CB00017B/2424